FLORA

CENTER FOR PHOTOGRAPHIC ART

# KATHLEEN BARROWS  FLORA

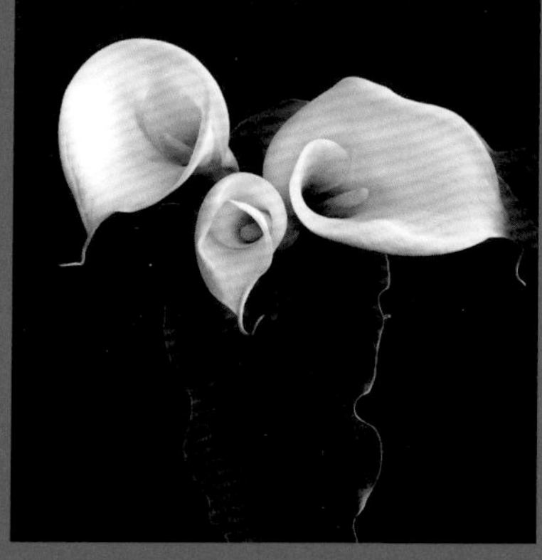

Introduction by
**KAREN SINSHEIMER**

Foreword by
**DENNIS HIGH**

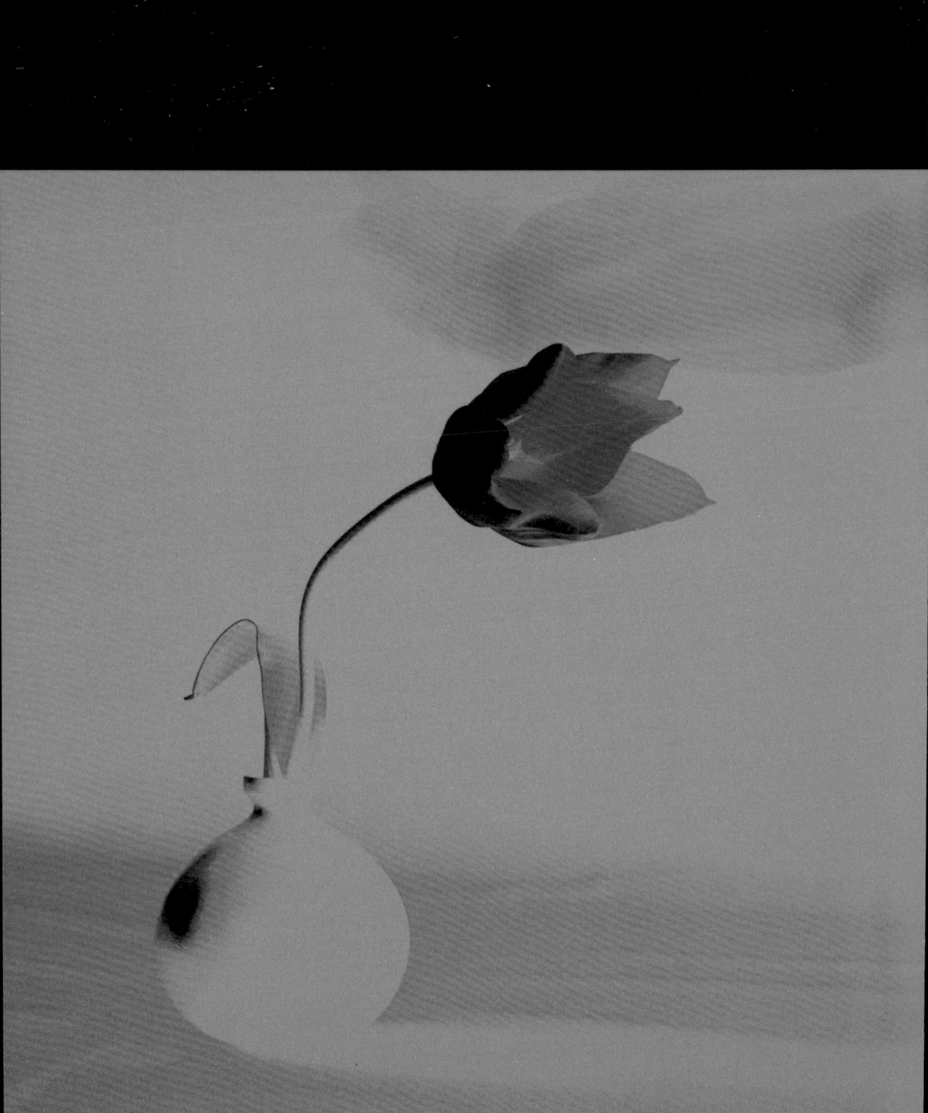

There is always a challenge in finding a way in which one can express the artistic elements which reside in all of us. Some start this quest at birth. Others envision that this process is an integrated part of our day to day life. These daily bits and pieces of creative flow surface with or without being consciously acknowledged or otherwise acted upon. Then there are those who have been found to cultivate their creative self much later in their life, a path less traveled but none the less worn.

The latter occupants of this list of scenarios had, for one reason or another, only brief moments of creative clarity, a yearning not yet developed during their younger years, when life seemed all consuming. But there is an up side to the late life epiphany when it comes to those who are overcome with the passion of art making, they are motivated by the ticking of the clock to finish what they have meant to say all their lives. There is a depth to their work, a patina, which covers layer after layer of self realized purity.

*Flora* is a monograph of quiet intensity. It originates from a woman who made a commitment, as a mature adult, to seriously explore the possibilities of photography as her creative voice. Her mentors during this process have been some of the finest photographers of our day but it was her inner sense of play and exploration, combined with a keen creative eye that kept her moving forward, producing this inspiring body of work presented in this intimate monograph.

There are millions of us who are approaching the latter part of our life's journey. Perhaps we can see ourselves as Kathleen Barrows has, that the clock is ticking, making it more the reason to look at what we can contribute creatively and let our voices be heard as Kathleen has so eloquently shown us hers.

Dennis High
Executive Director/Curator
Center for Photographic Art
Carmel, California
September 2003

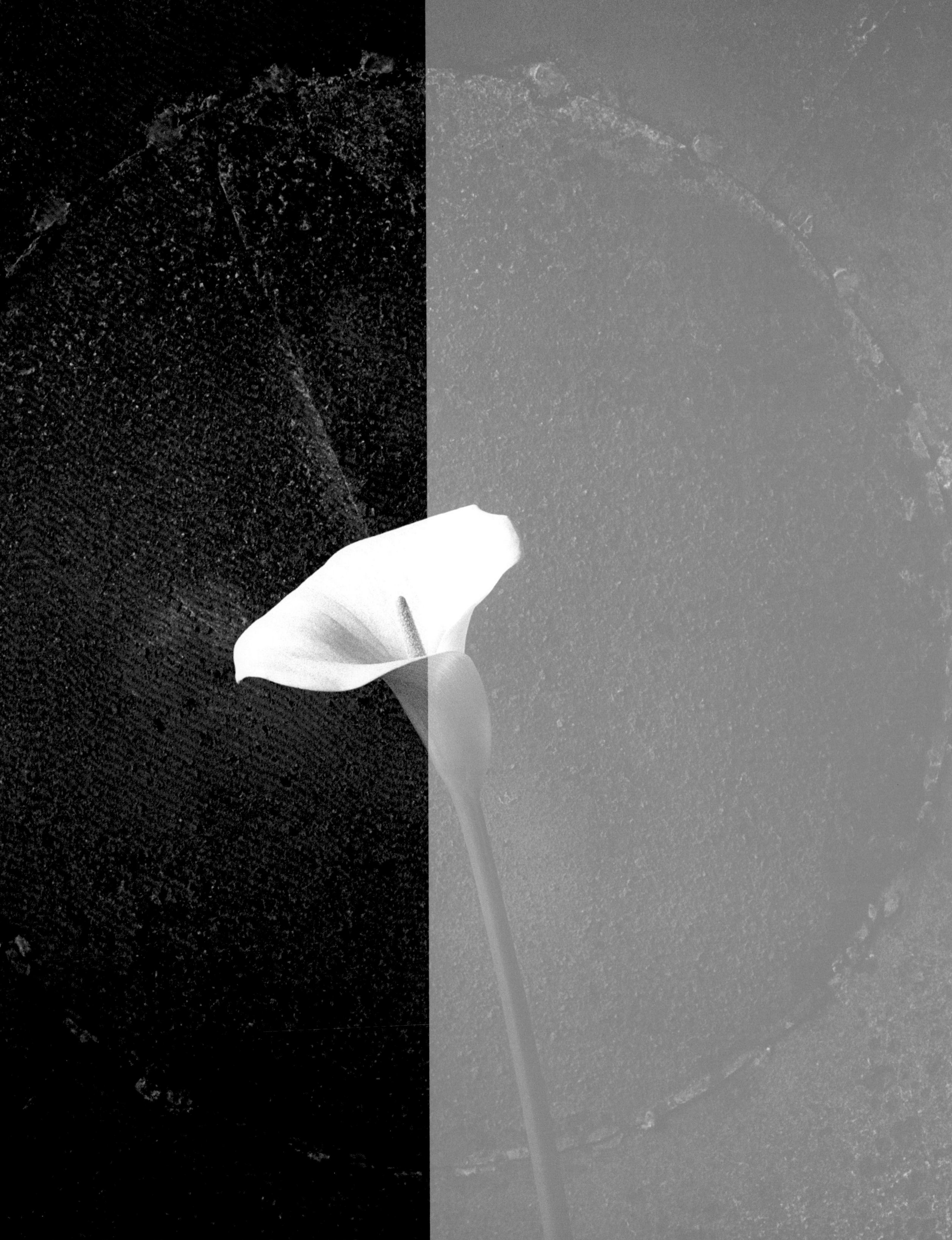

Imagine the determination with which Kathleen Barrows, a shy, young girl of eleven years, boarded a public bus in Richmond, Virginia. The year was 1936 and her destination was a camera shop. She put her two dollars on the counter and put an Argus A on layaway, returning to make monthly payments until the camera was her own. The cost of the camera was roughly $12.50, but that first purchase marked the beginning of a seven-decade commitment to photography.

Kathleen doesn't credit a specific event or moment that sparked her lifelong pursuit of photography. The artist's first camera was a Brownie and it became a very good friend, giving her the confidence to go anywhere. From the moment she took possession of the Argus A, making images has remained a constant in her life.

Her father, although not a photographer, assisted her in rigging up a camera as an enlarger. The darkroom, next to a coal bin, opened an unlikely world of exploration where she could lose herself for hours as she printed her photographs. She signed the back of her first print in pencil, suggesting the serious commitment that has proved to be true.

Kathleen began by photographing family gatherings and occasions, her family and pets, and anything else that caught her attention. With her camera held at eye level she felt invisible and in control. A product of both her generation and upbringing, she found that photography provided an acceptable entree to a broader world within the confines dictated by the norms of the 1950s.

As a young woman, Kathleen Barrows assumed the expected roles of wife and mother but she never let go of her photographic pursuits. For a time she became a businesswomen, but even in the midst of multiple demands and stress, she continued her photography. Working with a camera nourished her spirit as she dealt with daily necessities.

While meeting the needs of her growing family throughout these years, she also protected and nurtured a special corner in her life dedicated to photography. Kathleen signed up for local photographic workshops to continue to learn and to photograph.

Kathleen had the constant encouragement and support from her husband, Austin. He was an ardent admirer of her creativity, always pushing her to become the artist he knew she had the potential to be. During this time, the Barrows hosted artists-in-residence who came to teach in workshops in the Monterey Bay area, including photographers such as Paul Caponigro, Lucien Clergue, and Phil Davis who stayed with them for several weeks at a time. Kathleen learned something from each of them; they became critics, teachers, and friends, as she continued to refine her own photographic vision.

World travels followed, allowing her to visit both familiar continental destinations as well as third-world countries. Her archive contains significant images from those years and places, and over the course of the past six decades, Kathleen has produced an impressive number of images.

But during the years when travel and time were limited, or familial needs and obligations were pre-eminent, Kathleen explored a world of infinite variety in her garden. Just as Imogen Cunningham, with three boys to raise and a portrait studio to run, focused on her garden, Kathleen Barrows found artistic challenge and sustenance in floral subjects. Every home she has ever lived in has been graced with a bouquet of fresh flowers, and flora continues to be a provocative photographic subject.

Thus, this first, elegant book of Kathleen Barrows photographs is devoted to images of flowers, which in many ways reflect the artist's contemplation on her own life. There are lush, full portraits of a peony and iris in full bloom, where the light seems to radiate both to and from the subject, and three perfect calla lilies full in form. A backlit sunflower, turning its face away, emanates power and resilience while the close-up portrait of a delicate, multi-petaled rose, lying against a cracked, peeling surface, underscores softness and vulnerability.

There is lightheartedness as well. A young tulip, its stem a gawky curve, is open, racing toward the sunlight. In another calla lily image, the elegant form seems to stride into the picture with grace, like a beautiful woman who commands the room the moment she enters.

The quiet pictures reveal other aspects of Kathleen's vision. A single, perfectly formed bud stands in dignified solitude, its spine straight, reaching toward the light, while another nascent bud, partially revealed in slat-fingered light, is poised to achieve its full promise.

Most poignant, perhaps, are the images of flowers decaying and dying. A calla lily, mottled and marred, still retains some of its former beauty, while another has finally surrendered, its weathered and papery dark skin near collapse. The Dying Horse, once a bouquet of French tulips, has dissolved into a chaotic tangle.

Flora is not a new subject but it is an enduring one. Throughout the ages, artists have created images of flowers, and, from the moment an image could be fixed on paper, photographers were no exception. For Kathleen Barrows, flowers have provided a continuous source of exploration and contemplation.

The images offered here are personal, intimate gems, reflecting the artist's lifelong pleasure and meditative moments in the company of flowers.

Karen Sinsheimer
Curator of Photography
Santa Barbara Museum of Art
September 2003

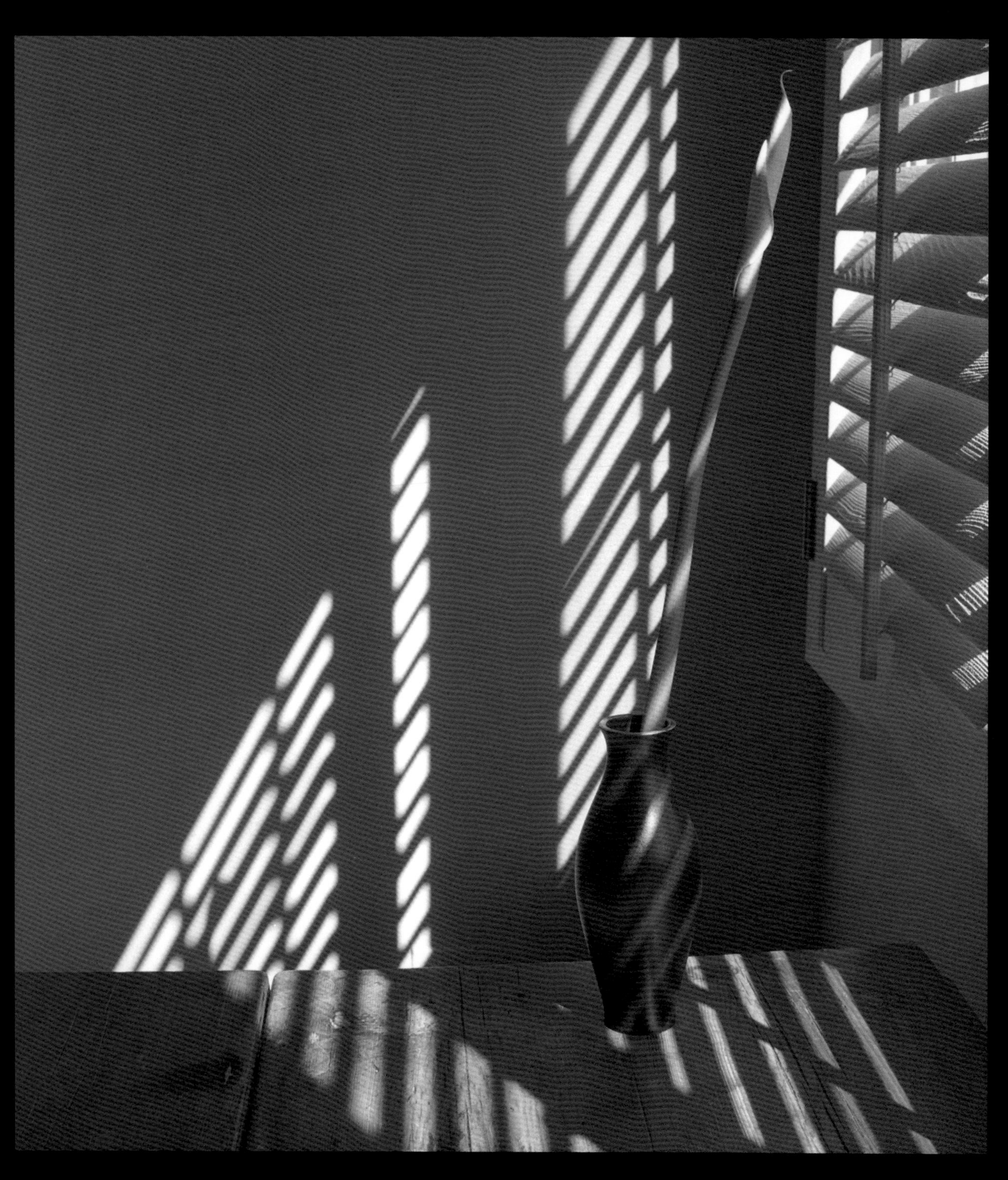

MINOR KEY

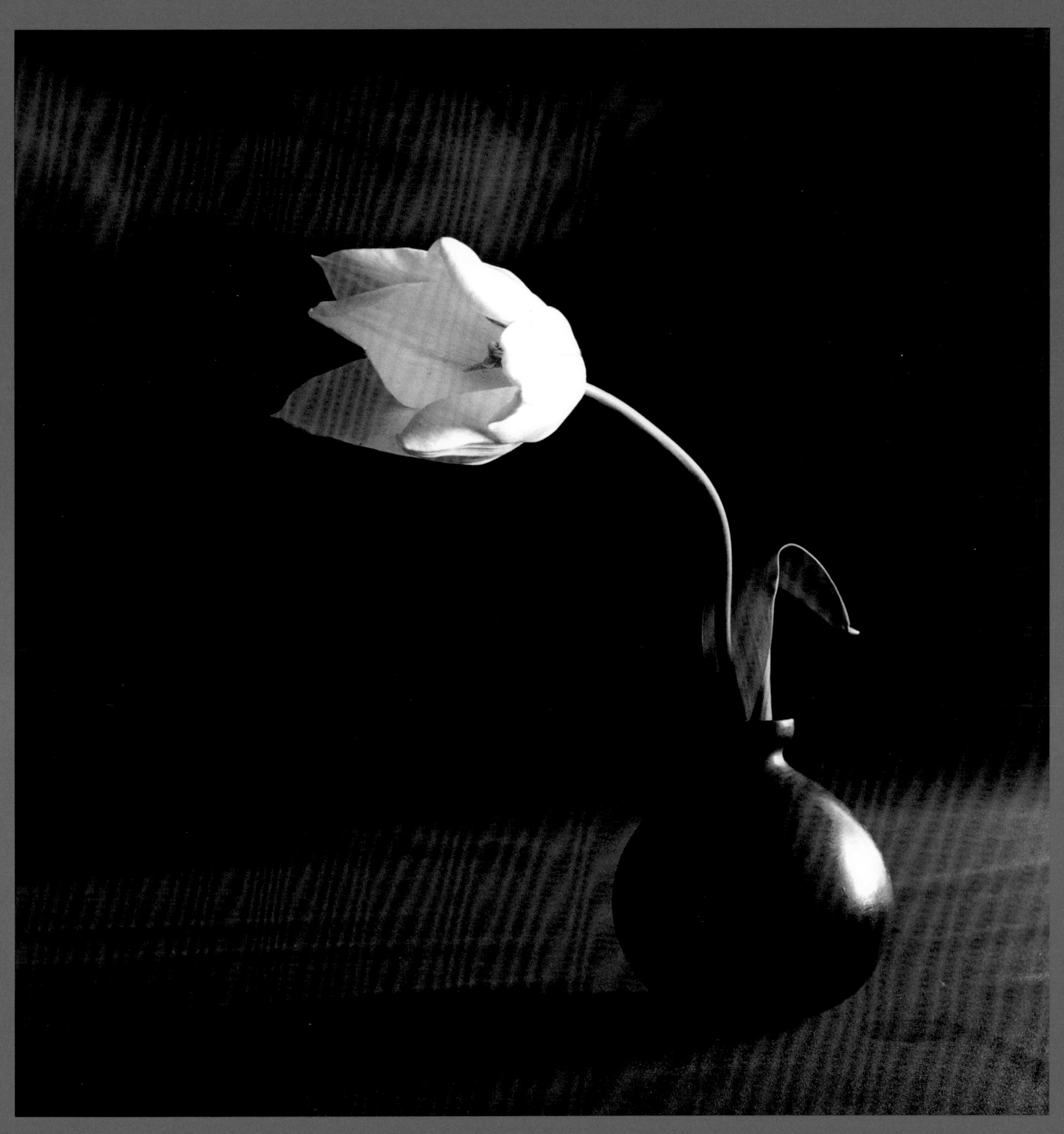

*The Dance* - 1 9 8 9

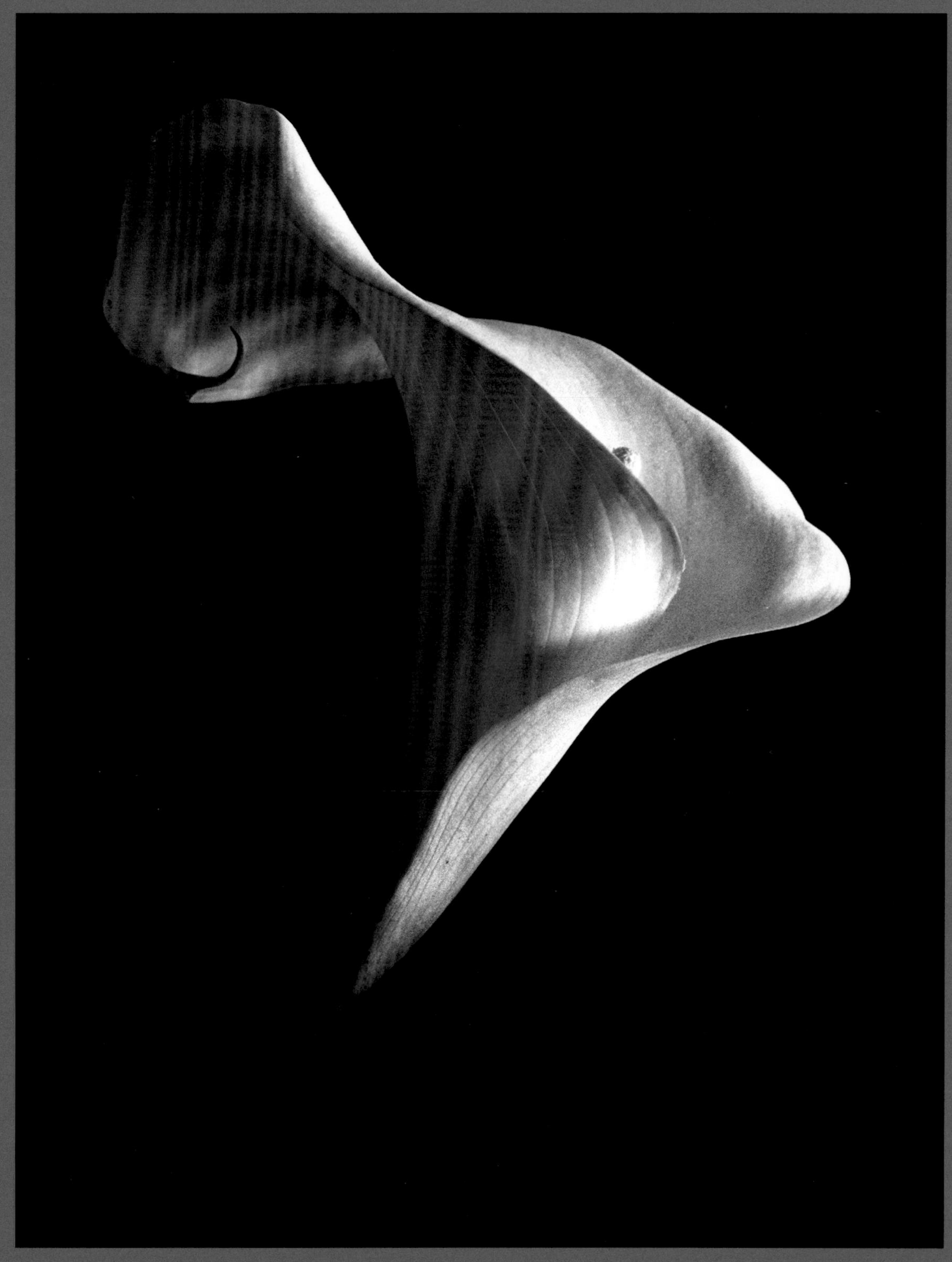

*Tulip Detail*

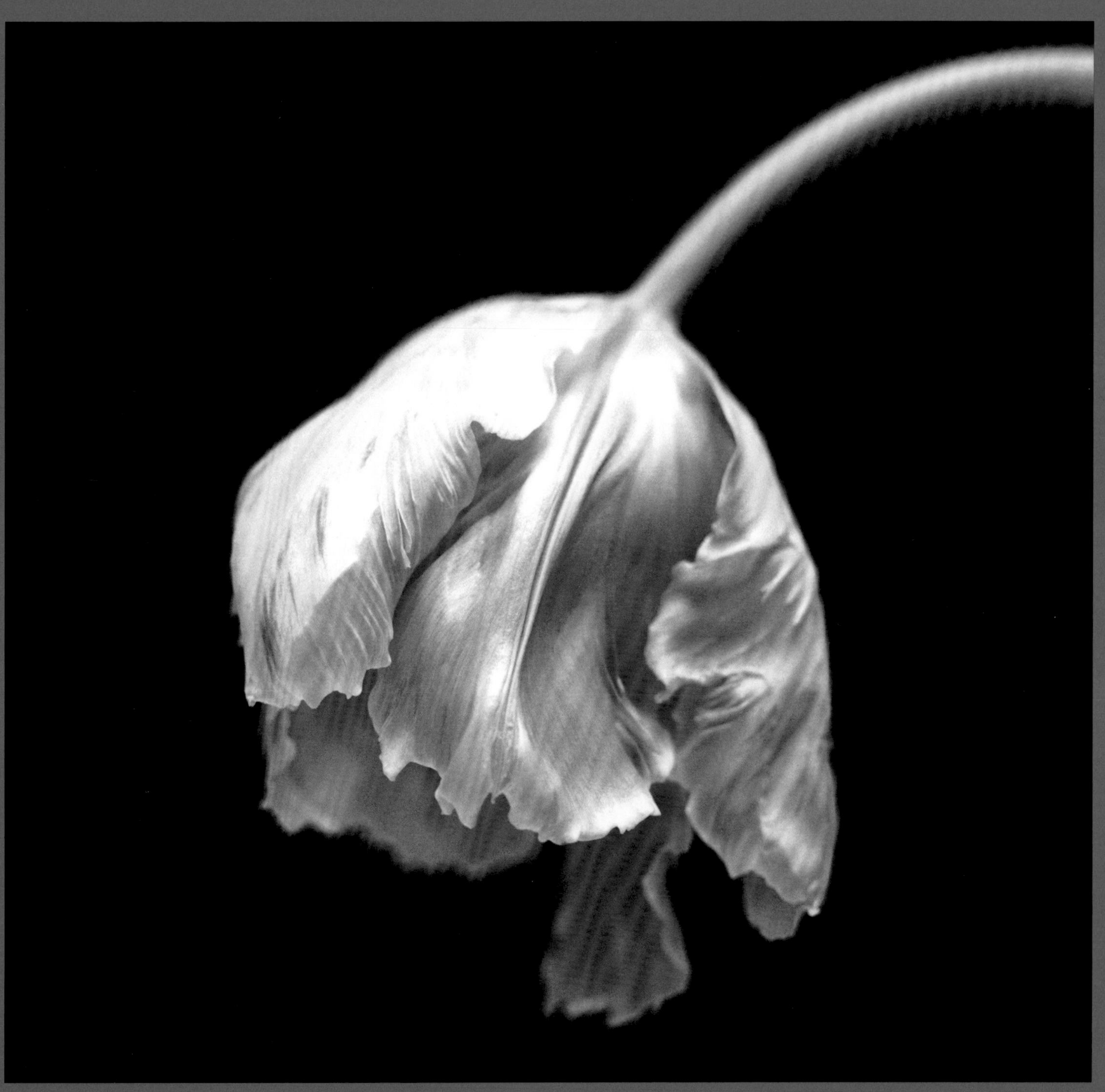

*Magnolia*

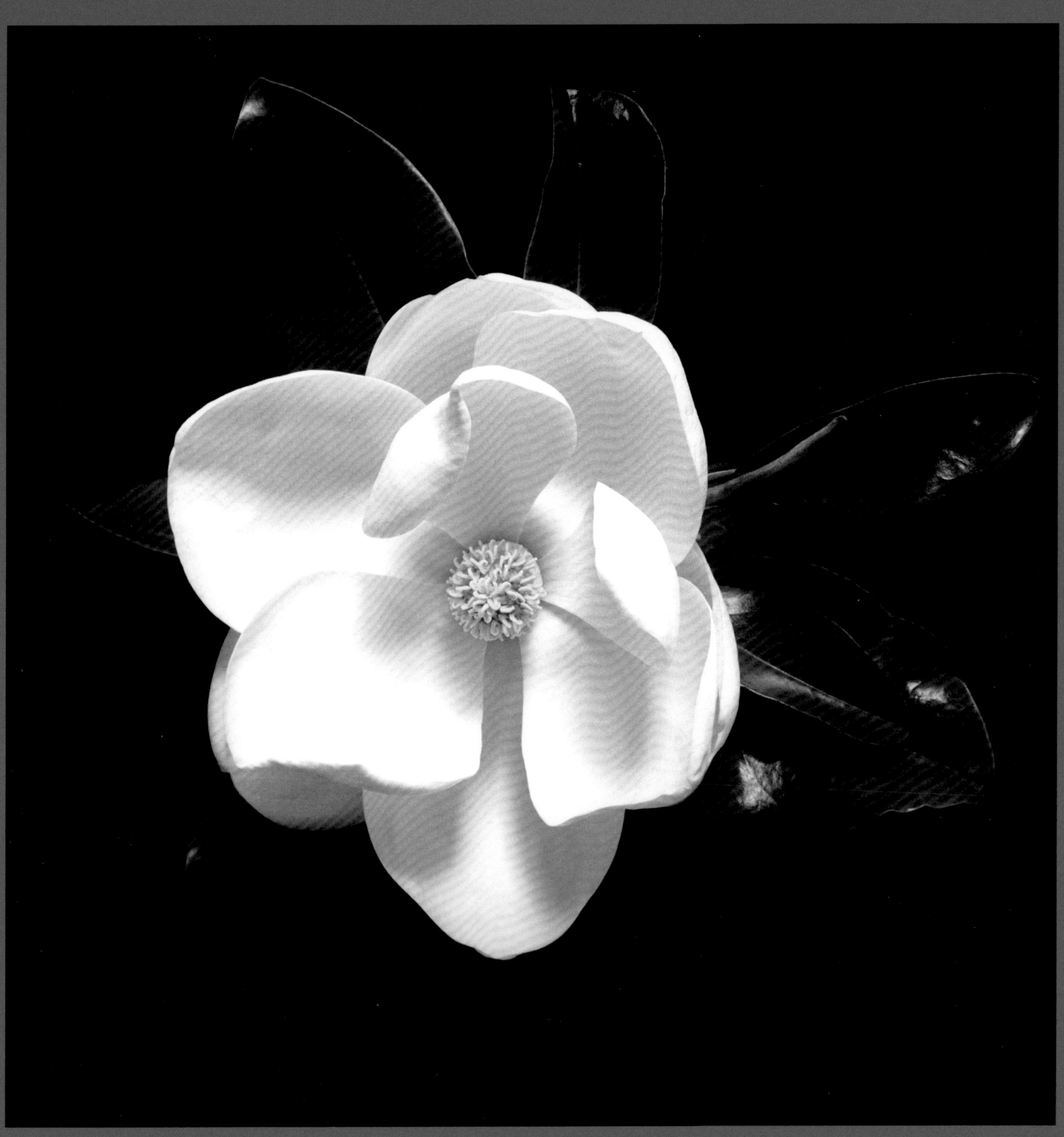

*Calla Duo*

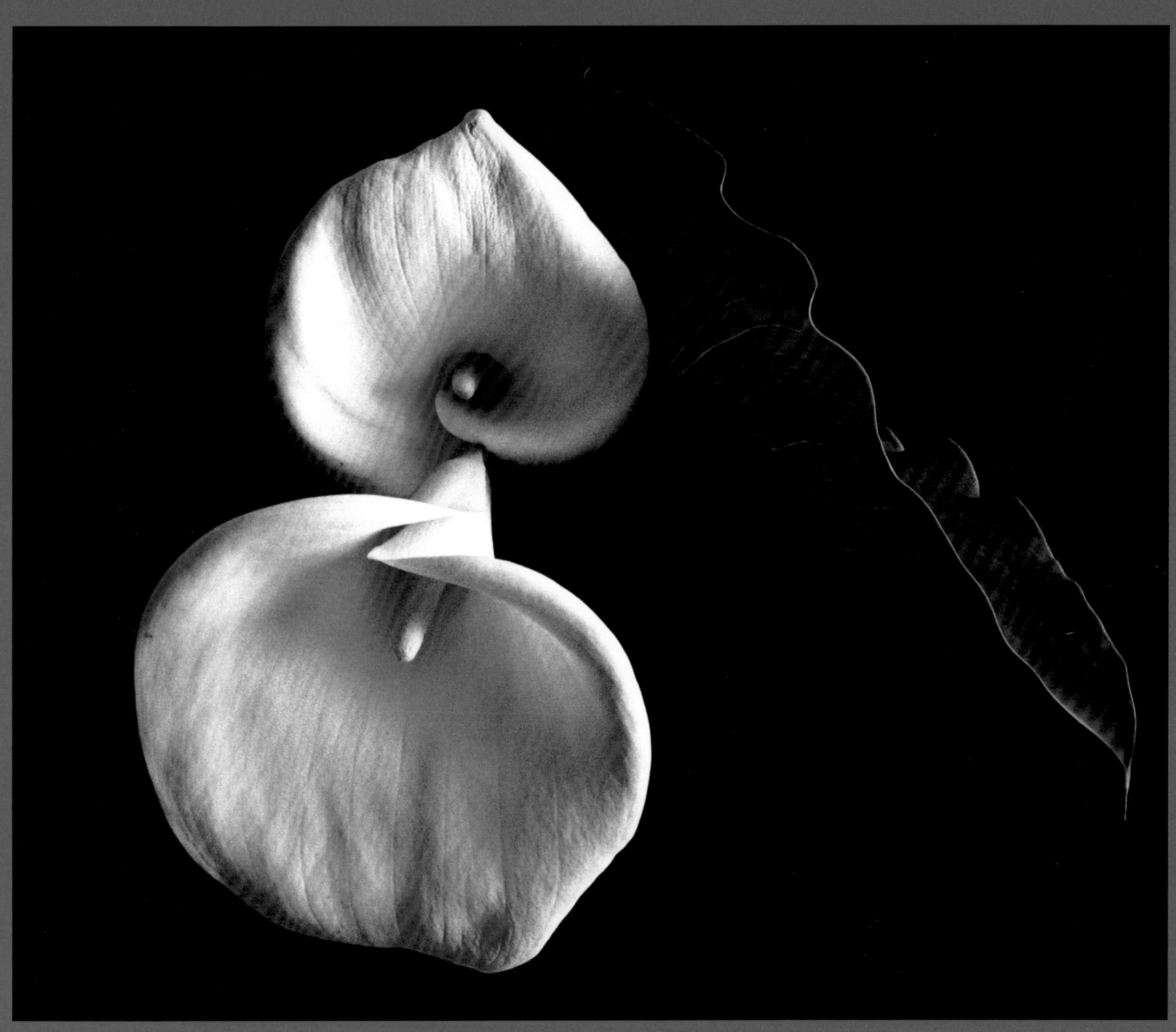

*Peony*

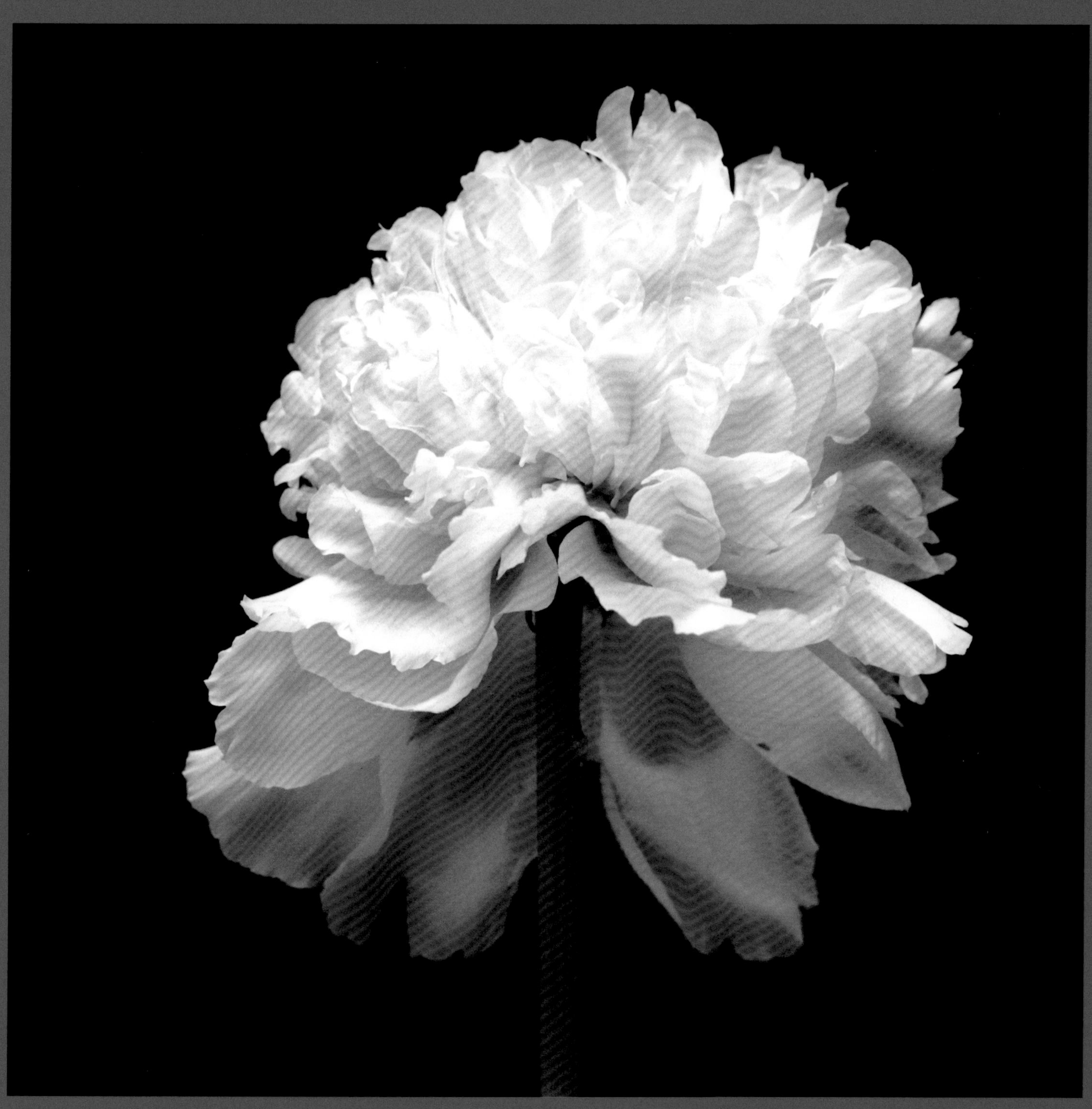

*Amaryllies – live and decayed*

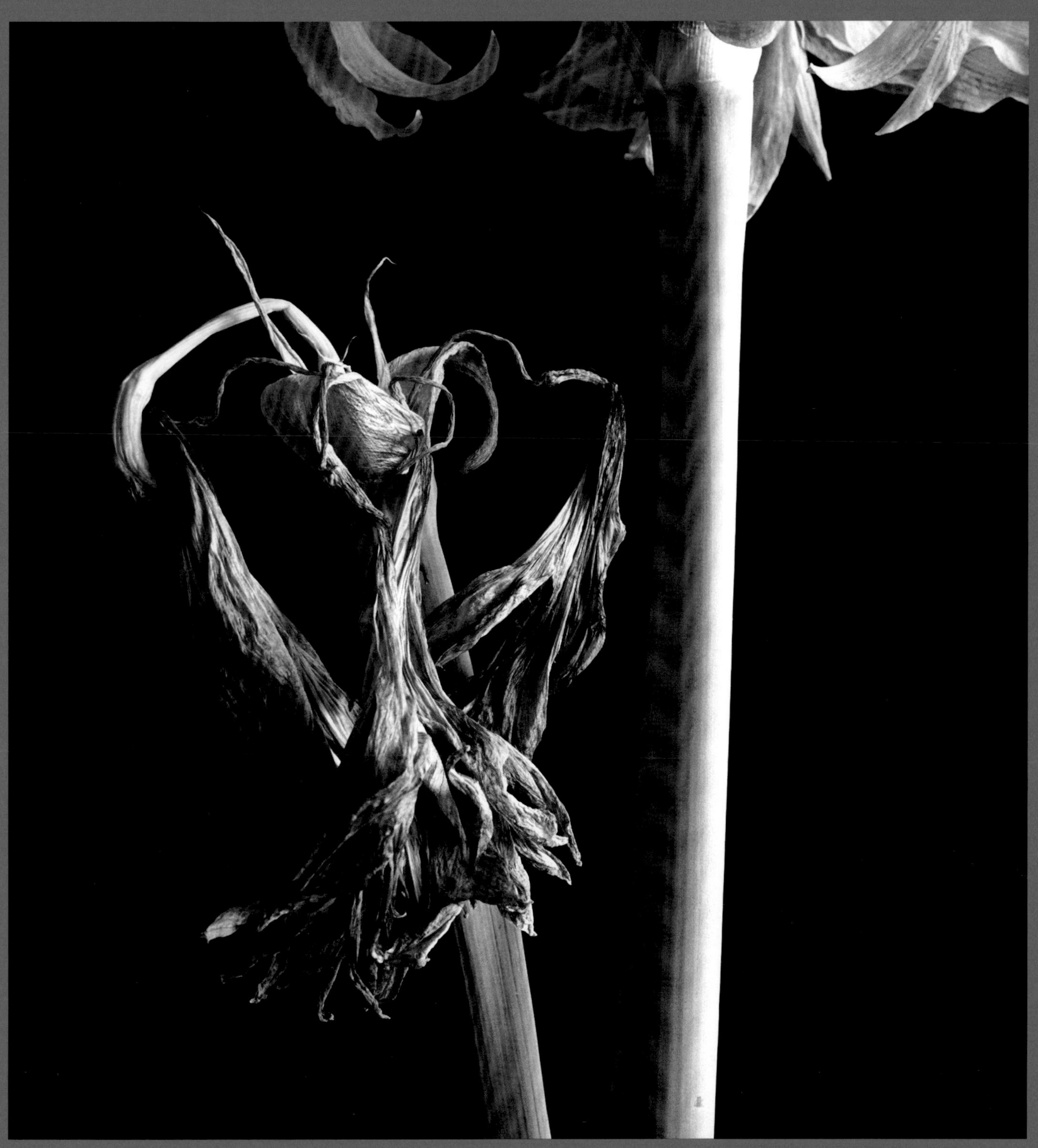

Dying Horse

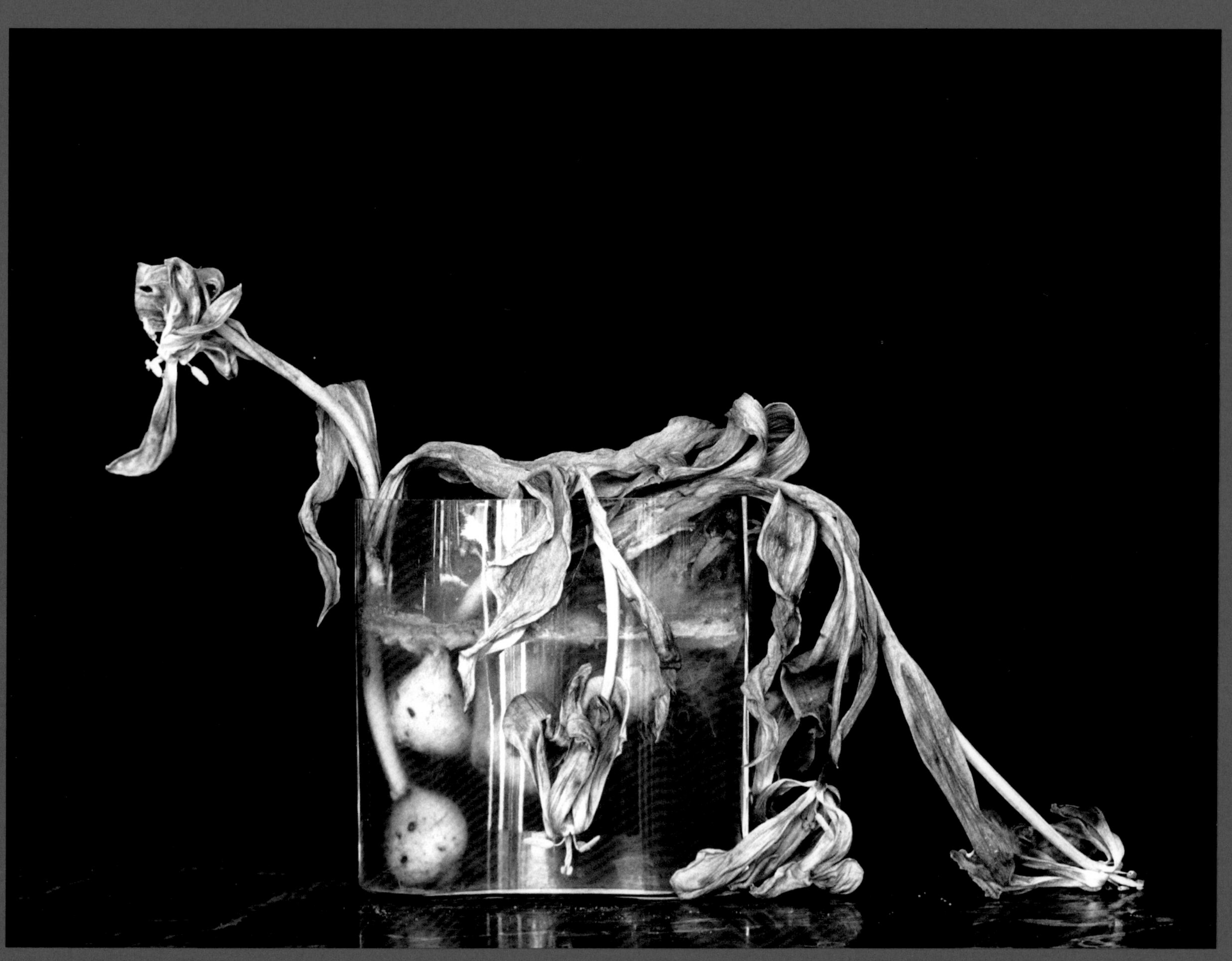

*Decayed Calla Lily*

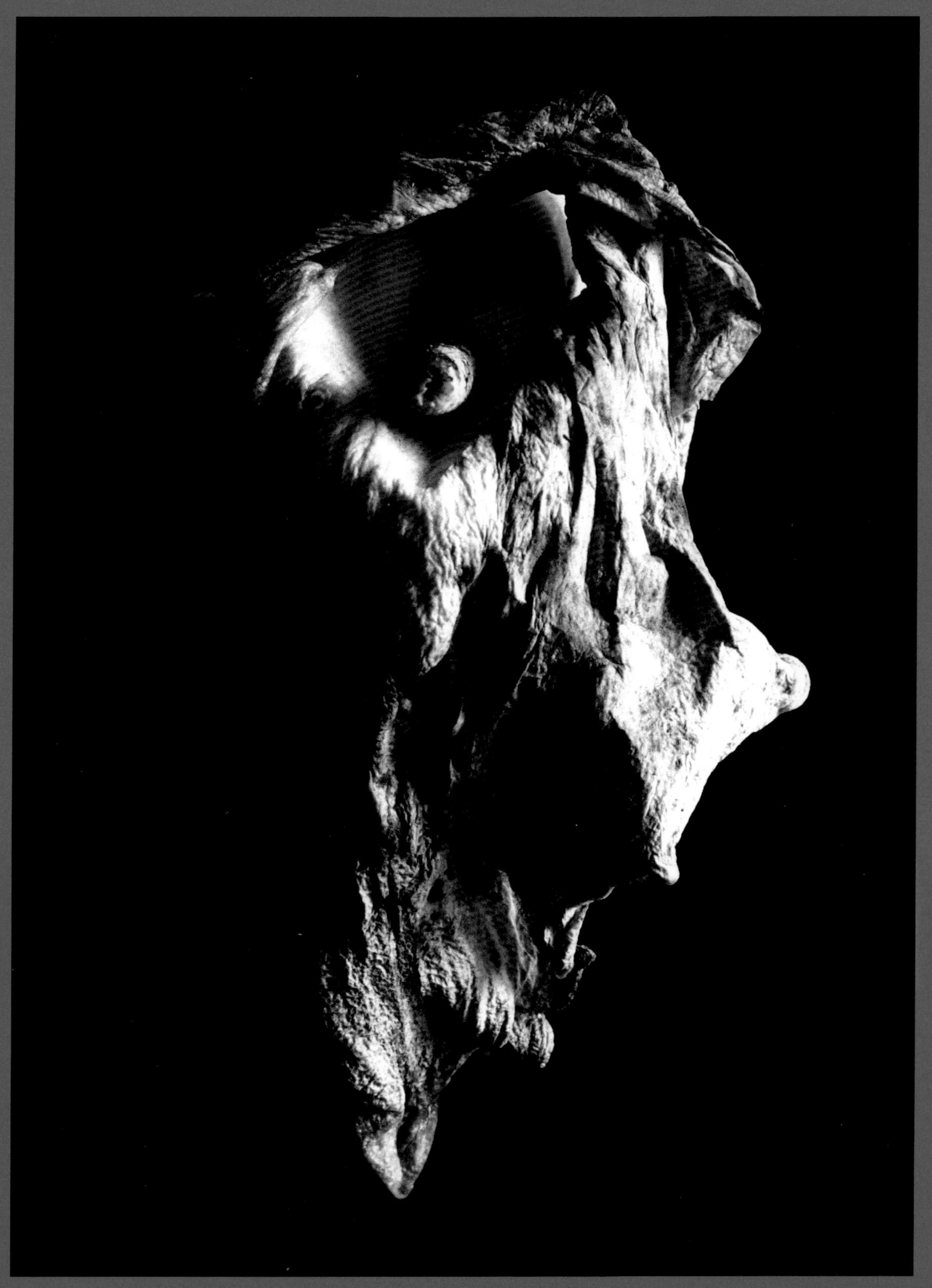

*S u n f l o w e r*

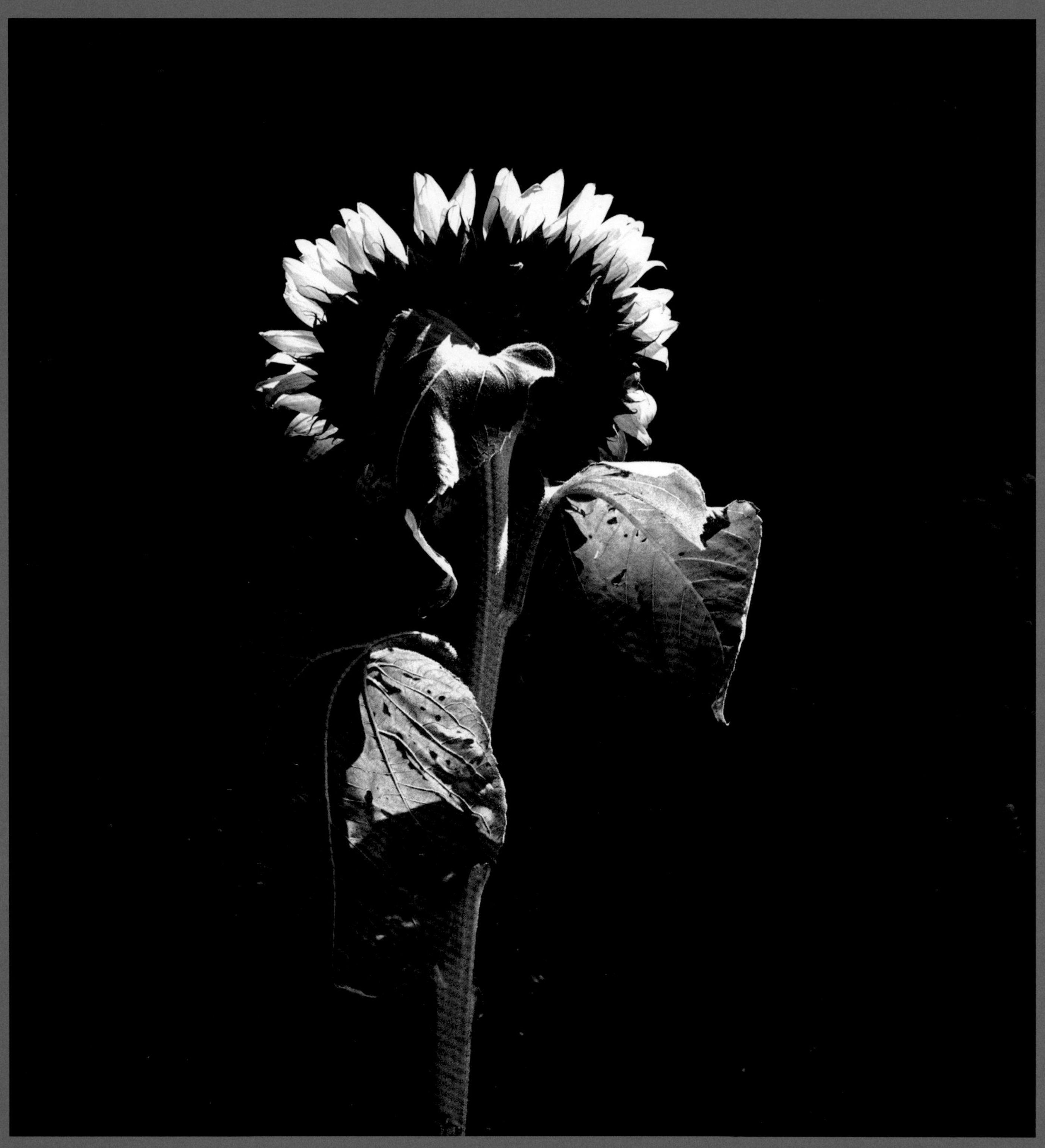

Dying Calla Lily

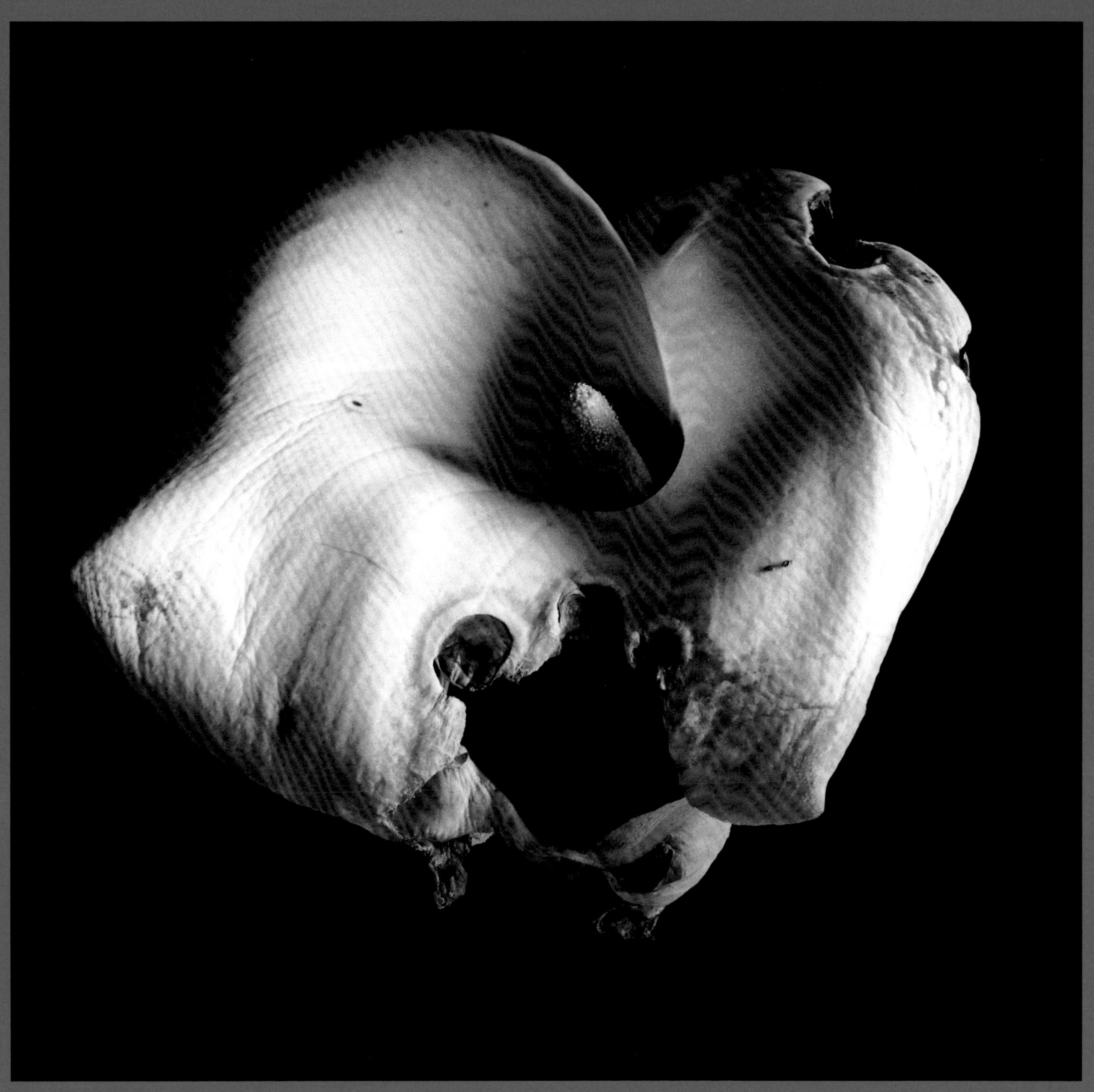

*Tulip*

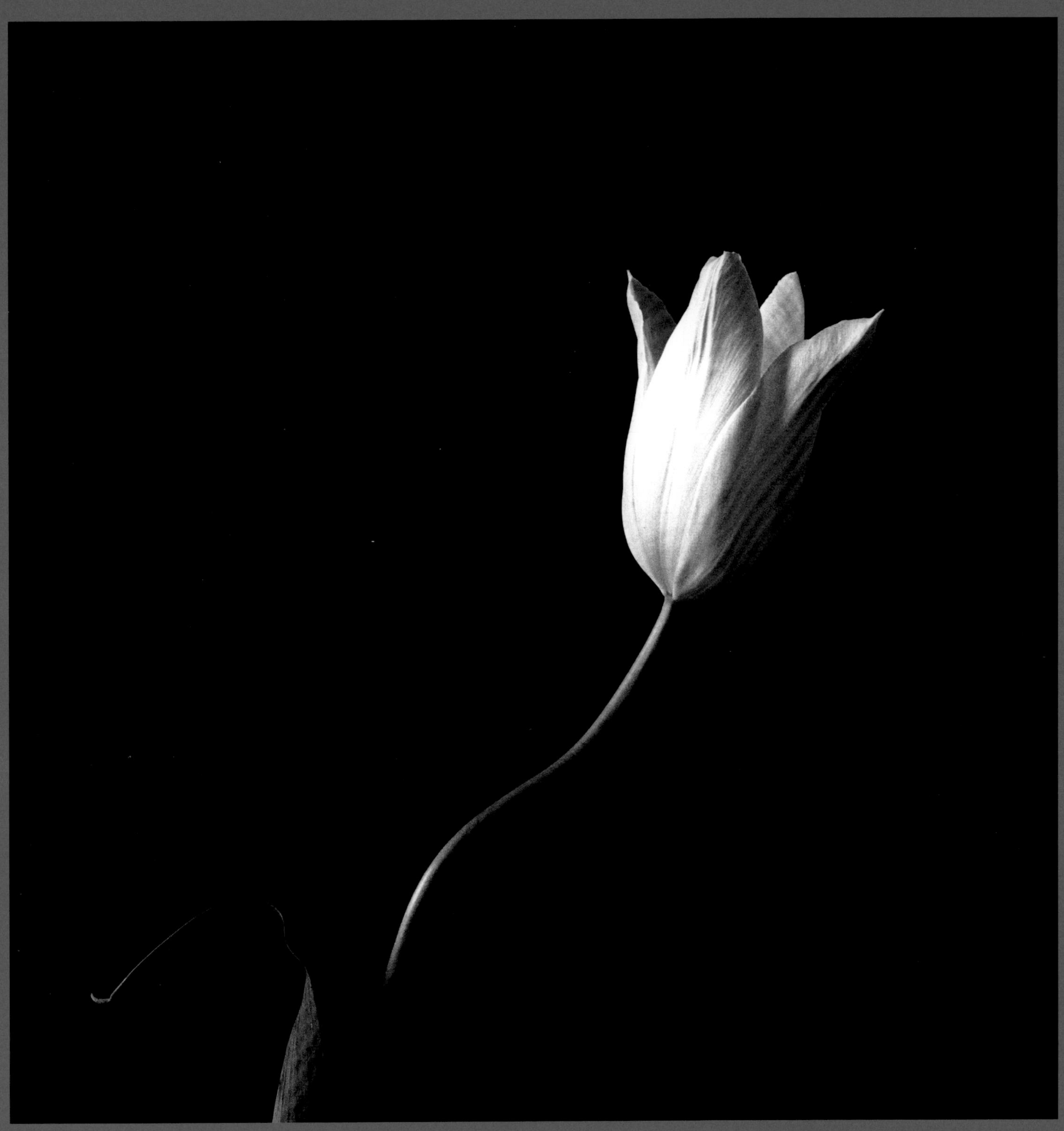

*F l o w e r s   a n d   I r o n   D o o r*

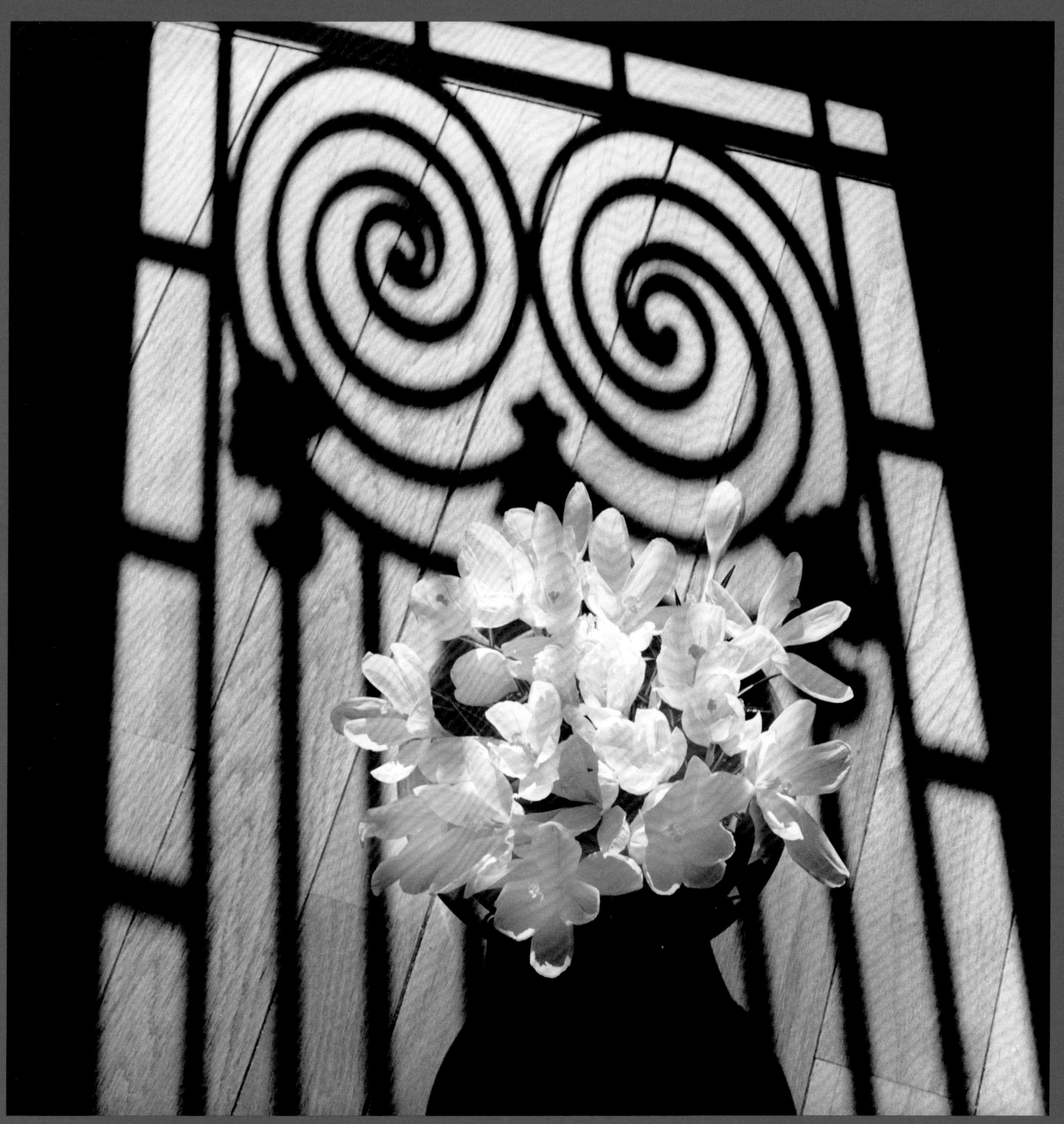

*Lilies Trio*

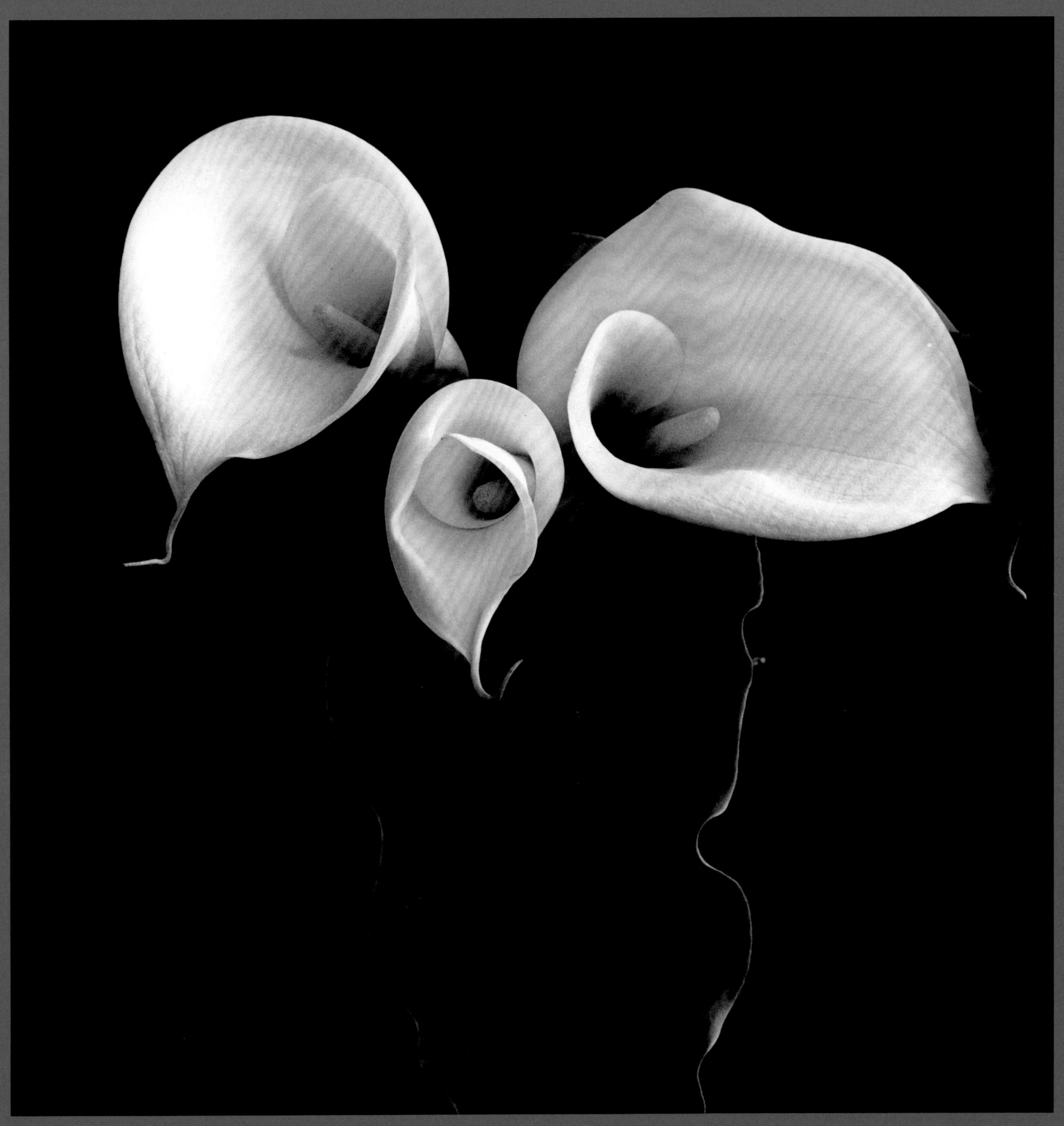

*Calla on Round Back*

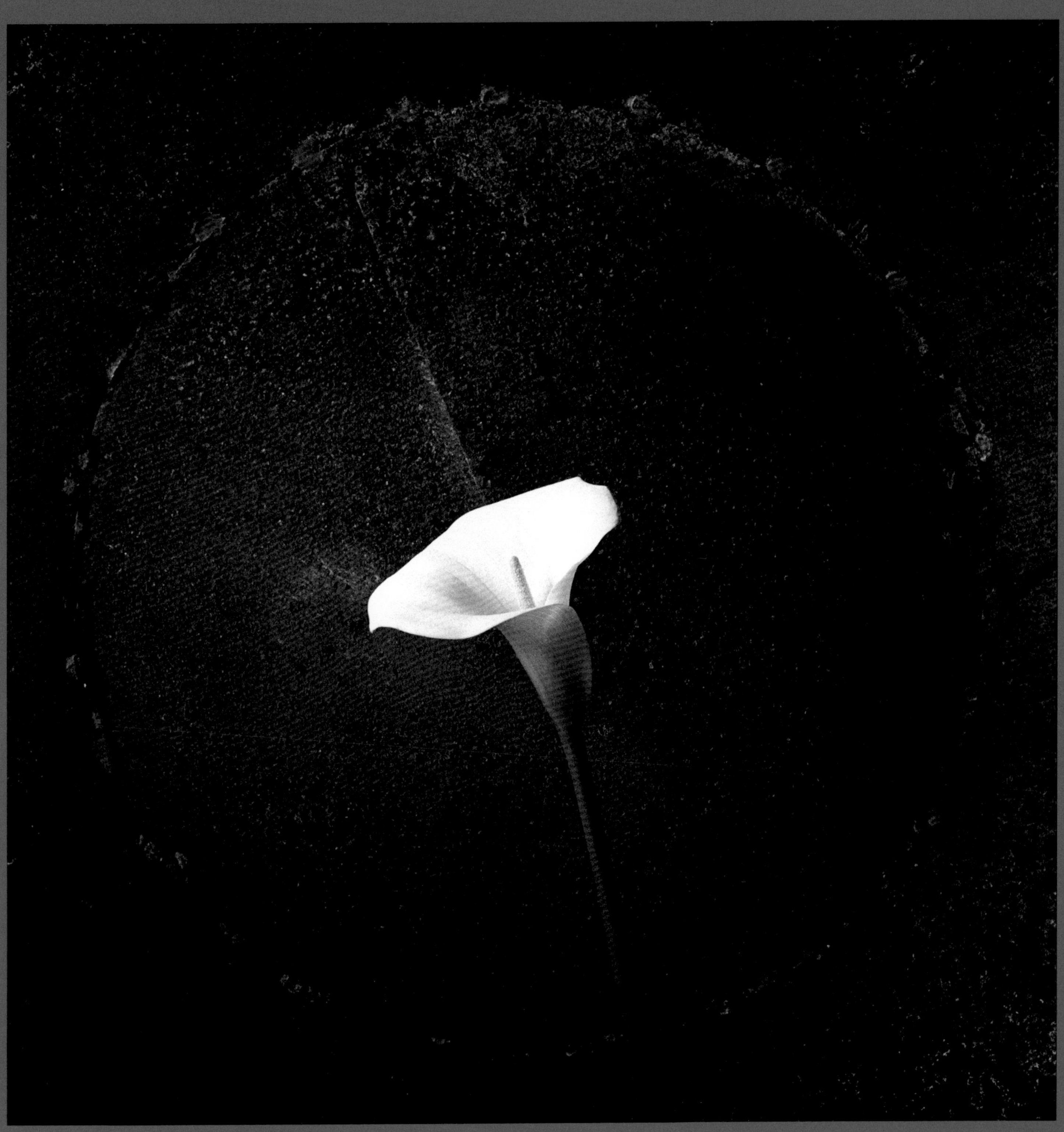

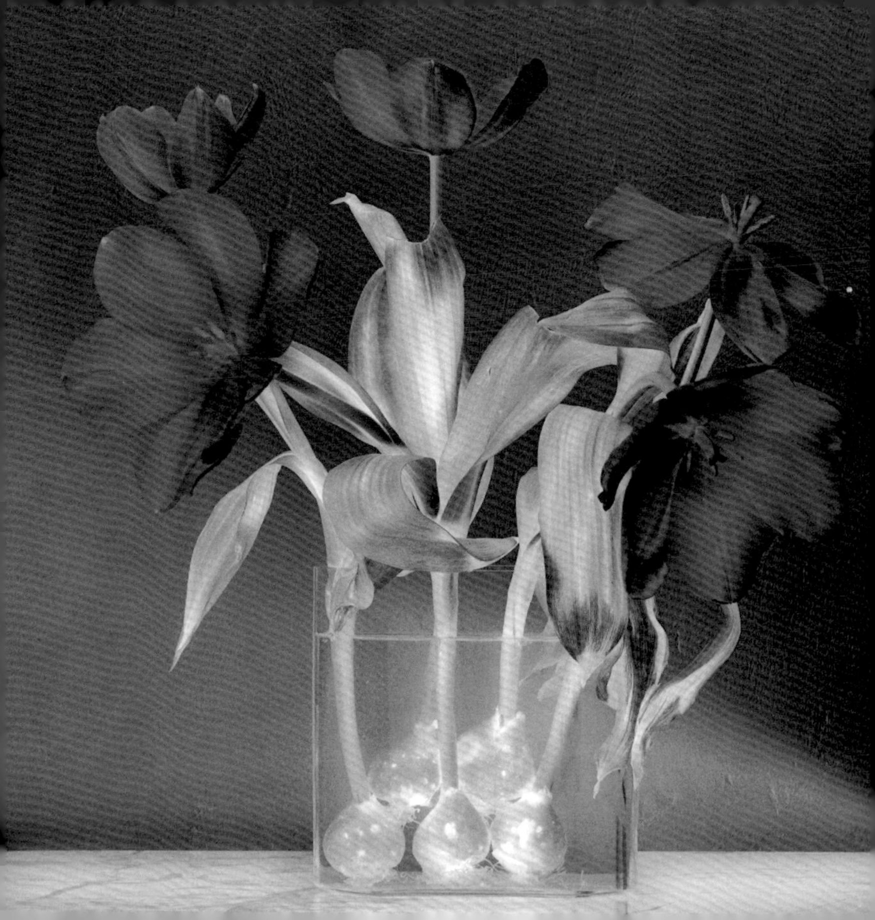

THE SCORE

*Amaryllies One*

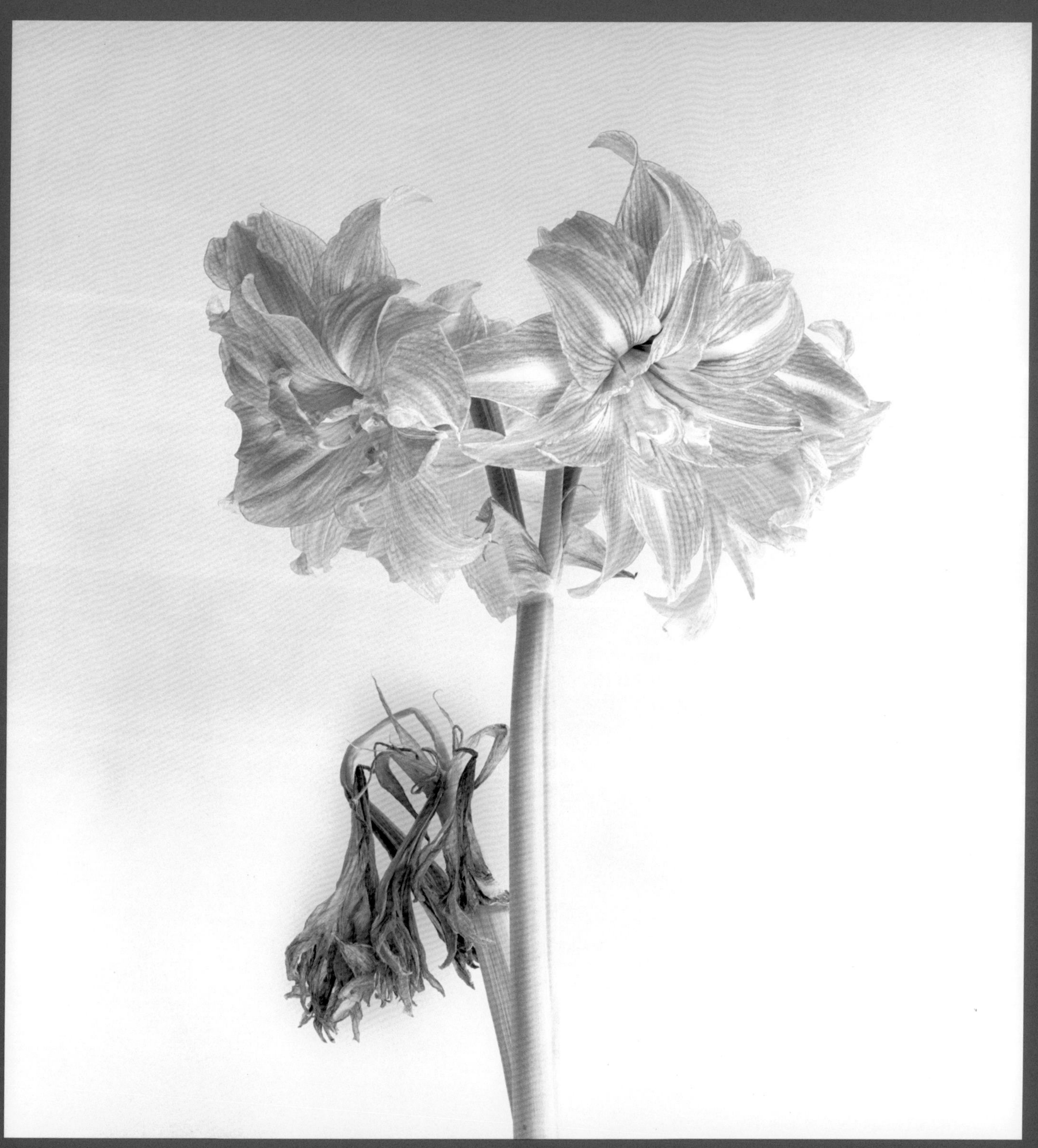

*B u l b s  —  R e g e n e r a t i o n*

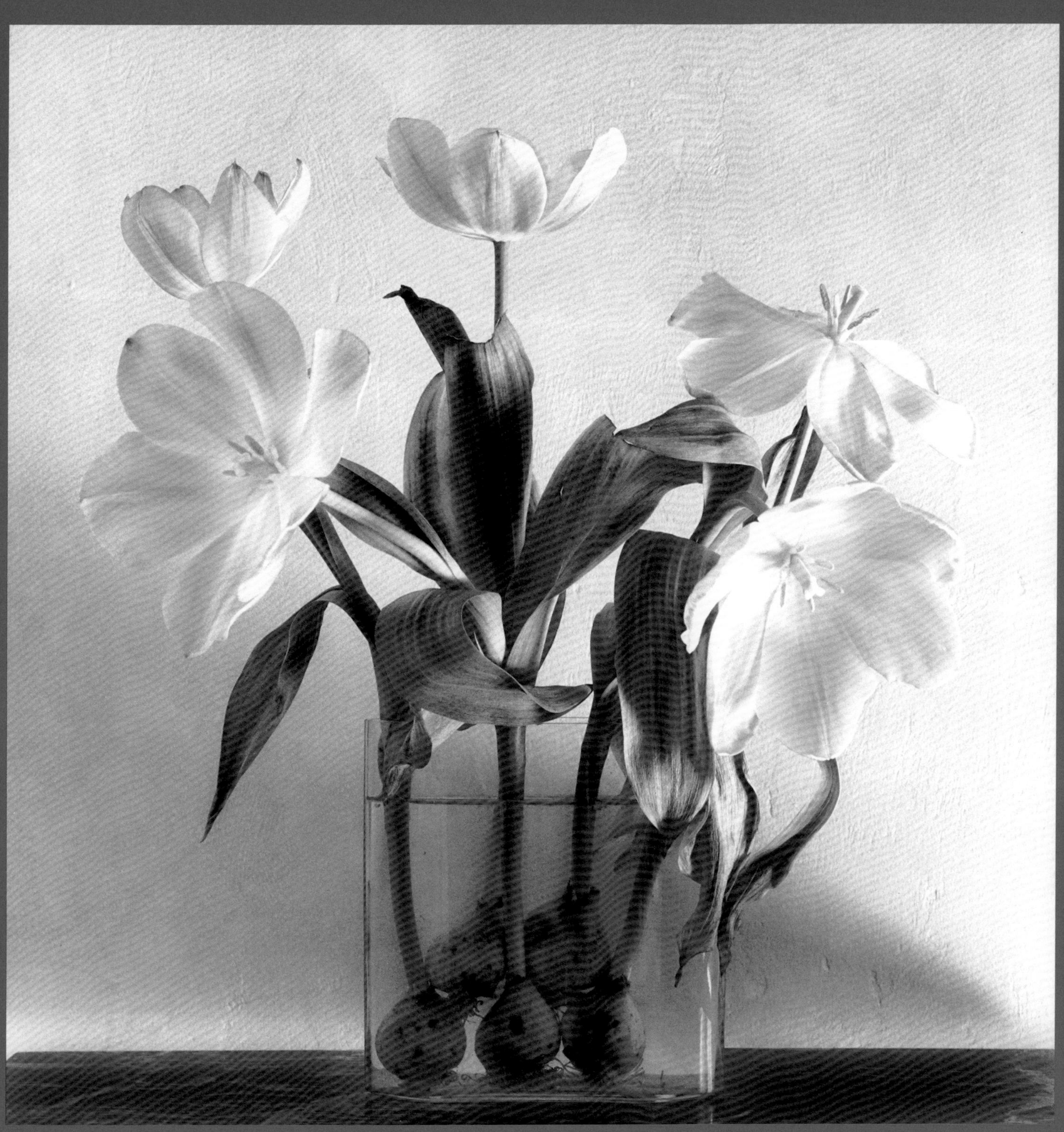

*Amaryllies – live and dead*

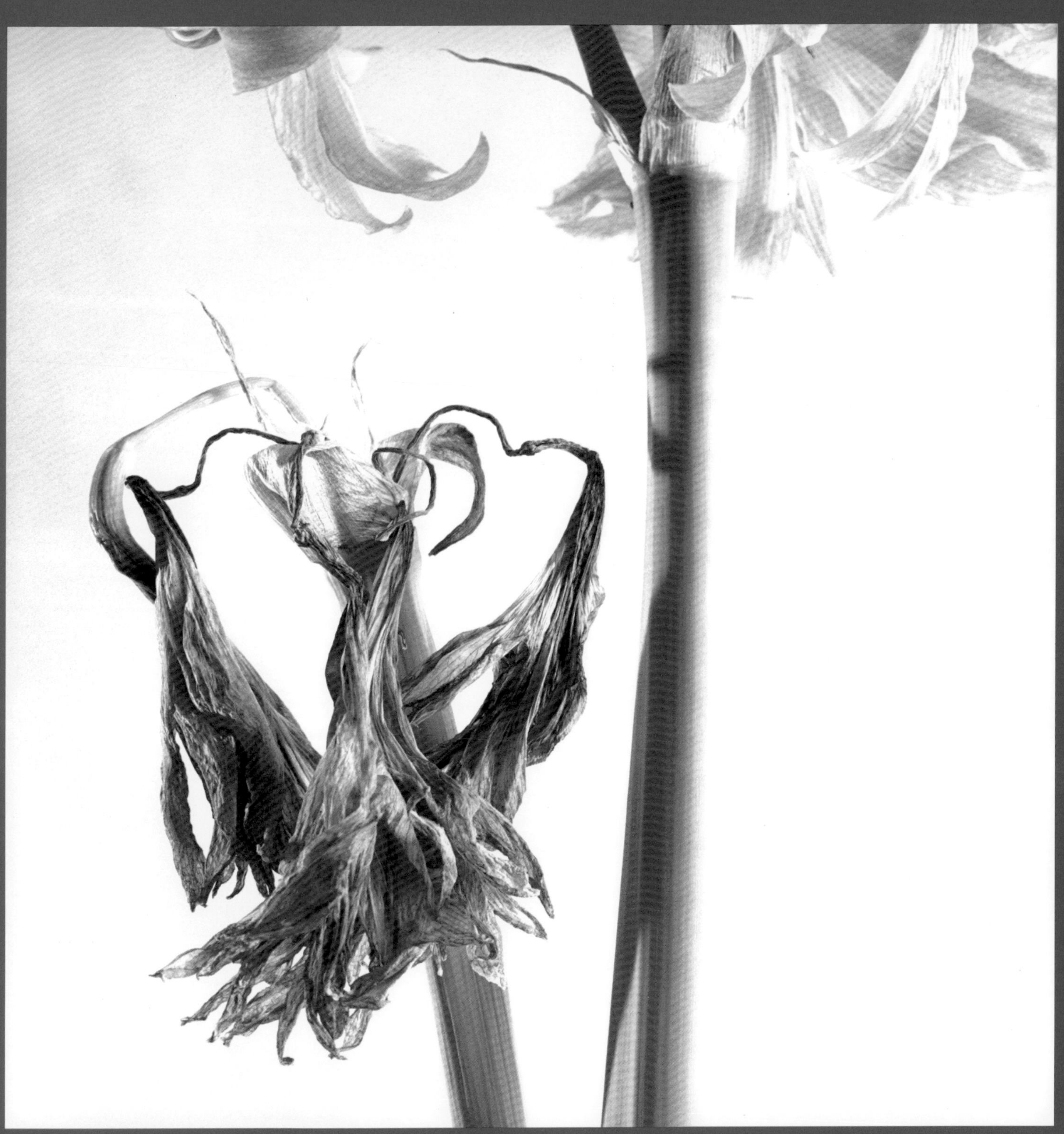

*White Rose Two*

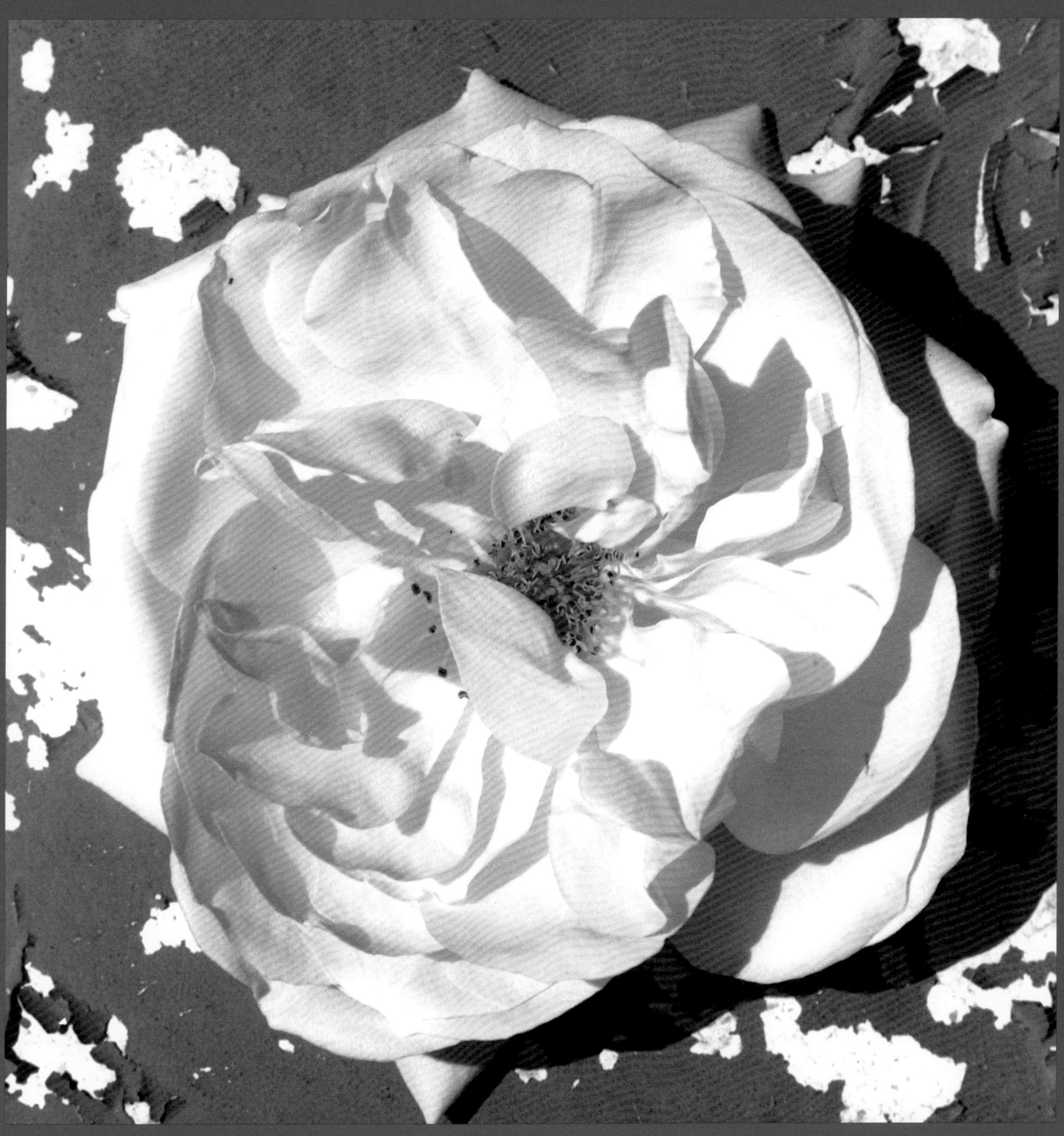

*White Rose*

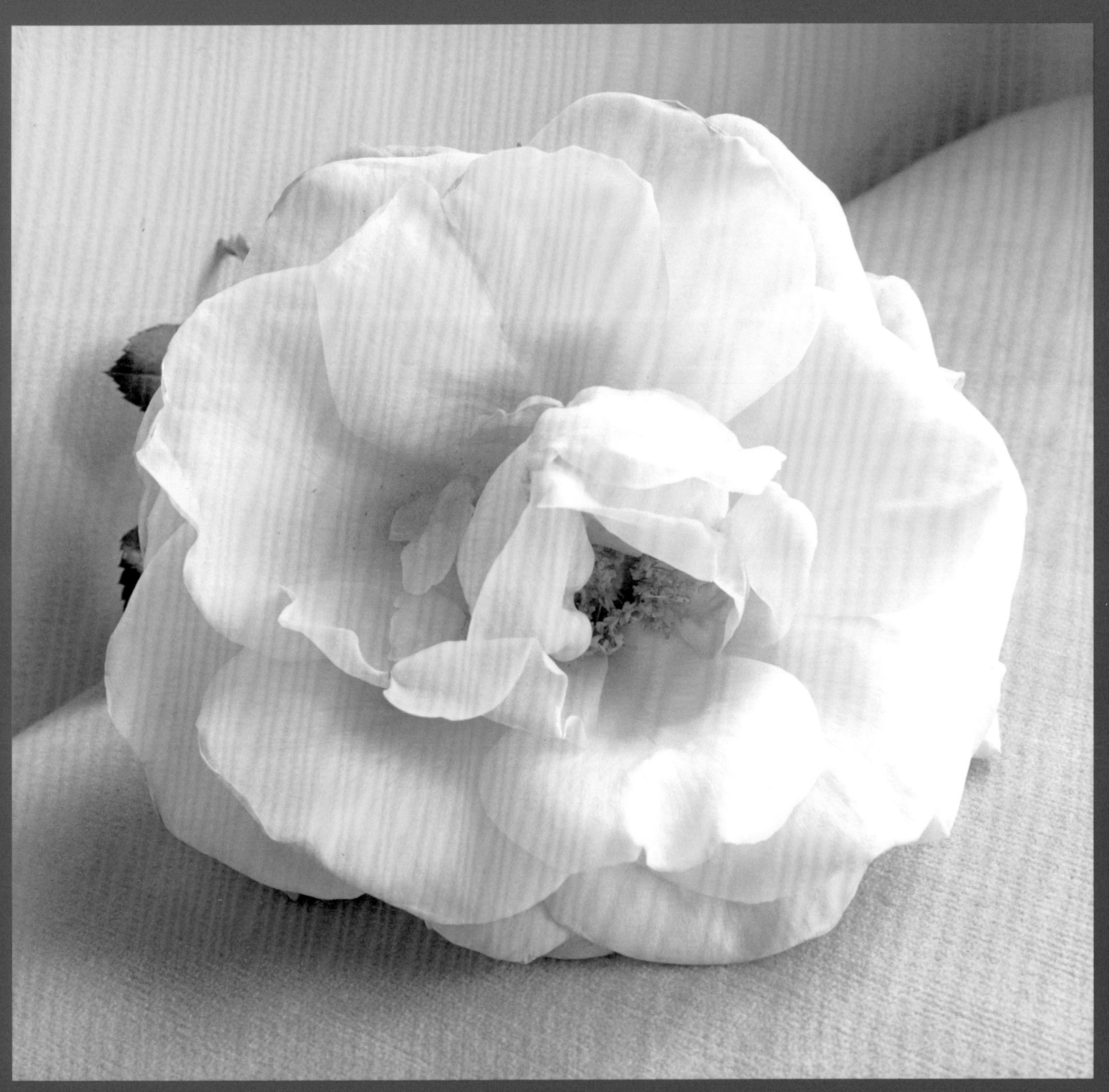

## ACKNOWLEDGMENTS

The path that led to this book literally began in my own
backyard when I was compelled to try and capture the
grace and temporal beauty of a handful of calla lilies.

I am indebted to *Dennis High* for guiding me towards
additional subjects to photograph and for introducing to
me many of the people who educated and supported
my vision. As my editor and as a dear friend, his art and
passion have informed and shaped this volume.

I would like to thank *Phil Davis* who taught me the
technical nuts and bolts of photography.

As a balance to the technical necessities of photography
I am grateful for the intuitive teachings of four individuals:
*Brad Cole,* who stimulated me to pursue the art and
passion of fine print making; *Elizabeth Opalenik,* whose
workshops inspired me to paint with light; *Paul Caponigro,*
who guided me to listen to the inherent voice in each
negative; and *Lucien Clergue,* who taught me to see the
softness at the heart of each photograph.

Thank you to B*arbara Vilander, Ph.D.* who not only keeps my negatives and prints organ-
ized, but whose love of the history of photography, I have come to know and to share.

I am grateful to *Karen Sinsheimer,* Curator of Photography at the Santa Barbara Museum
of Art, for writing the introduction for my book.

I have always enjoyed my family's support and encouragement and for that I am deeply
grateful. *Kathleen, John, Laurie Ann, Laurie* and *Mickey,* thank you. I will always cherish
memories of the subjects and props provided to me by Kathleen's daughters, *Amery* and
*Leigh Anne,* and for those moments we three shared in the darkroom watching prints
emerge in the developing tray. *Sean, Beau* and *Dominique,* bless you for sharing your
mother, *Laurieís,* sense of humor and playfulness in front of the camera. My love for all
of you is reflected in these photographs.

Finally, my most heartfelt thank you goes to my assistant, *Amilcar Garcia,* who is not only
my eyes, but also the expert in the digital storage and printing of my negatives.

To each of you I offer my deepest thanks and appreciation.

Kathleen Barrows
Santa Barbara, California
September 2003

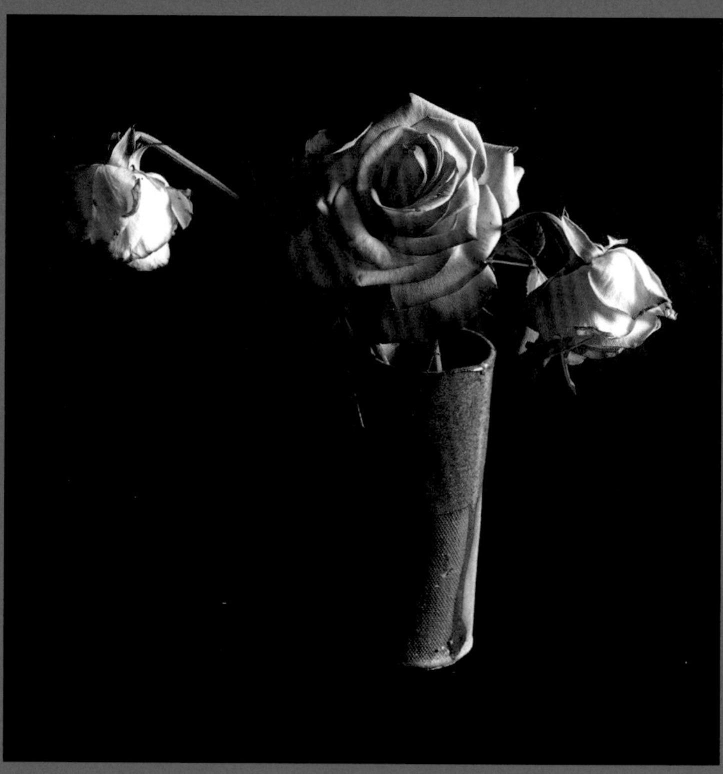

Library of Congress
Control Number
2003114191
ISBN 0-9630393-9

Design: Bert J. Ihlenfeld
Pacific Grove, California

Printed in China